RACIAL JUSTICE IN AMER
INDIGENOUS PEOP

GAINING
U.S. CITIZENSHIP

HEATHER BRUEGL

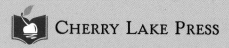

Published in the United States of America by Cherry Lake Publishing Group
Ann Arbor, Michigan
www.cherrylakepublishing.com

Reading Adviser: Beth Walker Gambro, MS, Ed., Reading Consultant, Yorkville, IL
Cover Art: Felicia Macheske

Produced by Focus Strategic Communications Inc.

Photo Credits: © ASSOCIATED PRESS, 5, 13; © mark reinstein/Shutterstock, 7; Library of Congress Prints and Photographs Division, 9, 16, 17, 22, 23, 27; Hulton Archive, Public Domain, via Wikimedia Commons, 11; © A21sauce via Wikimedia Commons, CC BY-SA 4.0 DEED, 15; © zimmytws/Shutterstock, 19; The National WWI Museum and Memorial, 21; © Heather Bruegl, 25; Lawrence Jackson/The White House, U.S. Department of the Interior via Flickr, CC BY-SA 2.0 DEED, 28; © arindambanerjee/Shutterstock, 30; © Teko Photography, 31

Library of Congress Cataloging-in-Publication Data

Names: Bruegl, Heather, author.
Title: Gaining U.S. citizenship / by Heather Bruegl. Oneida Nation of Wisconsin/Stockbridge-Munsee. Other titles: Gaining United States citizenship
Description: Ann Arbor, MI : Cherry Lake Publishing, [2024] | Series: Racial justice in America: Indigenous peoples | Includes index. | Audience: Grades 7-9 | Summary: "The journey towards full citizenship was long and winding for Indigenous peoples in the United States. Readers will come to understand how legal status affected the lives and opportunities of Indigenous peoples throughout American history. The Racial Justice in America: Indigenous Peoples series explores the issues specific to the Indigenous communities in the United States in a comprehensive, honest, and age-appropriate way. This series was written by Indigenous historian and public scholar Heather Bruegl, a citizen of the Oneida Nation of Wisconsin and a first-line descendant Stockbridge Munsee. The series was developed to reach children of all races and encourage them to approach race, diversity, and inclusion with open eyes and minds"— Provided by publisher.
Identifiers: LCCN 2023043586 | ISBN 9781668937938 (hardcover) | ISBN 9781668938973 (paperback) | ISBN 9781668940310 (ebook) | ISBN 9781668941669 (pdf)
Subjects: LCSH: Indians of North America—Government relations—Juvenile literature. | Indians of North America—Legal status, laws, etc.—Juvenile literature. | Citizenship—United States—Juvenile literature.
Classification: LCC E93 .B887 2024 | DDC 323.1197—dc23/eng/20231010
LC record available at https://lccn.loc.gov/2023043586

Cherry Lake Publishing would like to acknowledge the work of the Partnership for 21st Century Learning, a Network of Battelle for Kids. Please visit Battelle for Kids online for more information.

Printed in the United States of America

Note from publisher: Websites change regularly, and their future contents are outside of our control. Supervise children when conducting any recommended online searches for extended learning opportunities.

Heather Bruegl, Oneida Nation of Wisconsin/Stockbridge-Munsee is a Madonna University graduate with a Master of Arts in U.S. History. Heather is a public historian and decolonial educator and travels frequently to present on Indigenous history, including policy and activism. In the Munsee language, Heather's name is Kiishookunkwe, meaning sunflower in full bloom.

Chapter 1
**What Does It Mean to Be
a U.S. Citizen?** | Page 4

Chapter 2
**History of Indigenous
Citizenship** | Page 8

Chapter 3
**History of U.S. Relations with
Indigenous Peoples** | Page 14

Chapter 4
**Changing the Legal Status of
Indigenous Peoples** | Page 20

Chapter 5
Indigenous Politics Today | Page 26

Extend Your Learning | Page 32

Glossary | Page 32

Index | Page 32

What Does It Mean to Be a U.S. Citizen?

Hundreds of millions of people live in the United States. **Citizenship** is a legal classification. Living in the U.S. does not automatically make someone a citizen. People born in the U.S. and those who have American-born parents are citizens of the U.S. But how is being a citizen different from just living here?

Everyone who lives in the United States is governed by the U.S. Constitution, which means that everyone has protected rights. Everyone has the right to free speech and the right to practice their own religion. They also have a responsibility to pay taxes and follow laws. Citizenship provides other rights. The right to vote is one of these rights. U.S. citizens can register to vote when they are 18 years old. Voting is an essential right, but it is also a responsibility. It means that your voice is being heard and that your opinion is counted. Voting is what makes the U.S. a country *for* the people and *by* the people. U.S. citizens can also run for office and hold some federal jobs that require citizenship.

Other rights of citizens include safety from being deported. The U.S. government cannot legally deport its citizens. U.S. citizenship also lets people travel abroad with a U.S. passport. One hundred and eighty countries around the world welcome travelers with U.S. passports without requiring a visa. U.S. citizens can also get help from U.S. embassies in foreign countries. They can qualify for federal benefits such as food, housing, and tuition assistance, as well.

Today, Indigenous people like Mildred James of Navajo Nation, shown here, are full citizens of the U.S., with all its rights and protections.

Lastly, U.S. citizens have a responsibility to serve on juries. Juries help to decide court cases and to ensure there is equal justice under the law.

Who can be a U.S. citizen has changed over time. When the U.S. was a new country, many people were left out. Enslaved people were not granted citizenship, nor were their rights protected. Instead, they were legally treated as property. Indigenous people were denied citizenship as well and were often legally treated as enemies. Even as the U.S. grew across the continent, the Indigenous people who lived within its borders had few rights and even fewer protections. They were not allowed to be part of the nation founded on the land they loved.

The United States is a representative democracy, or republic, which means that citizens elect people to represent them. These elected representatives form the government. It is their job to make decisions that their voters agree with. If they fail to do this, they often are not reelected and lose their jobs. Voting matters, and the right to vote is sacred in a democracy. No matter how a person chooses to vote, every vote counts.

CHAPTER 2

History of Indigenous Citizenship

Indigenous nations inhabited what is now the United States for thousands of years. They called this land Turtle Island. Each Indigenous nation had its own form of government, language, culture, traditions, and process of determining citizenship.

Family and **kinship** could determine your citizenship within an Indigenous government. Indigenous nations often included different clans. Membership in a clan was passed through the mother's side of the family in many nations. Indigenous women had a lot of importance in tribal citizenship because mothers gave life and passed on culture. People could become citizens of a nation by marrying into the tribe or clan, even without having any Indigenous background.

The earliest Europeans to arrive in North America had to negotiate with the leaders of local nations, such as Massasoit, shown here, of the Wampanoag Nation.

Family was very important, and becoming family granted citizenship. There was an "all are welcome" philosophy.

This same philosophy continued as Europeans began settling in North America. Fur traders, especially, joined Indigenous nations. They married Indigenous women and became part of Indigenous communities. They worked with their new kin, gained access to Indigenous trade networks, and brought furs back to Europe. Their children grew up in a mix of cultures.

European nations eventually started colonizing North America. They claimed different areas for themselves, even without owning the land and in complete disregard for the Indigenous peoples already living there. European rulers gave large parts of the continent to colonizers. The rulers issued charters for permission to settle North American land. The 13 original U.S. states were created in this way.

Trading posts existed throughout North America for hundreds of years.

Colonists arrived with families. They established European-style settlements. They did not often join Indigenous nations through marriage, though they did trade with them. They bargained for land but sometimes took it by force. British colonists made alliances with some Indigenous nations and fought with others.

When the United States declared its independence, Indigenous people were greatly affected. A few Indigenous nations fought alongside the U.S., but most sided with the British, who had promised to protect Indigenous land. When the war ended, however, the U.S. did not protect its Indigenous allies. Instead, it soon started a removal policy to strip Indigenous nations of their land and to remove Indigenous people from the country.

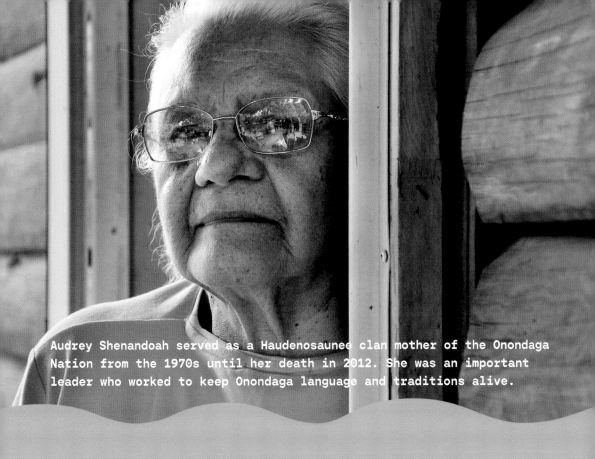

Audrey Shenandoah served as a Haudenosaunee clan mother of the Onondaga Nation from the 1970s until her death in 2012. She was an important leader who worked to keep Onondaga language and traditions alive.

Indigenous nations value the wisdom of women. Haudenosaunee women are an example of how Indigenous women often have essential roles in politics. The Haudenosaunee were originally a group of five unique Indigenous nations who formed an alliance and had a shared culture. Haudenosaunee clan mothers were in charge of agriculture and economics, and they were also the ones who voted for chiefs. Similarly, they could also remove chiefs who did not make good decisions. Many treaties had to be approved by the Haudenosaunee clan mothers, especially if land was involved. Clan mothers today are still vital parts of many tribal nations.

CHAPTER 3

History of U.S. Relations with Indigenous Peoples

The United States has a complicated history with Indigenous peoples. From the very beginning, policies have been in place that regulate the relationships between Indigenous nations and the federal government. In 1778, the United States signed its first treaty with an Indigenous nation, the Lenape. The treaty acknowledged the sovereignty of this Indigenous people.

In 1830, the U.S. government passed the Indian Removal Act. This act forced Indigenous people off their homelands. It made them move west of the Mississippi River into an area the U.S. government called Indian Territory. Treaties promised reservation land to Indigenous nations.

These reservations were considered separate nations, but the U.S. government also claimed to be in charge of them. The Indigenous people living there were not regarded as U.S. citizens. As a result, their rights were not guaranteed. They had no say in the laws that took away their land and ways of life.

Here, a Nanticoke Lenni-Lenape family attends an annual powwow in Delaware. Despite removal and broken treaties, the Lenape people and their culture have remained an important part of modern American life.

In 1887, the U.S. passed the General Allotment Act, which divided reservation lands into individual plots. The U.S. government wanted Indigenous people to live and act more European by farming on their own instead of as collective bodies.

Thousands of non-Indigenous settlers stormed Oklahoma for the chance to settle on Indigenous land. It became known as the Oklahoma Land Rush of 1889. Towns sprang up overnight. Another land rush soon followed in 1893.

The designated plots were assigned only to Indigenous people who registered, though, and any unassigned plots were considered "extra." The U.S. government sold this unassigned land to non-Indigenous settlers. Indigenous people could not protect their land because they were still not citizens and could not vote.

Some Indigenous peoples sued the U.S. government, and the case went to the Supreme Court. The Court ruled against the Indigenous peoples because it said they were not sovereign. Instead, the Supreme Court granted Congress the freedom to do whatever it wanted.

Later, the U.S. government passed laws to stop Indigenous peoples from practicing their religions. These laws showed that U.S. leaders did not think the Constitution applied to Indigenous peoples. But this would change as Indigenous people began to fight for their citizenship.

Section 1 of the 14th Amendment of the U.S. Constitution states, "All persons born or naturalized in the United States, and subject to the jurisdiction thereof, are citizens of the United States and of the State wherein they reside."

Section 2 includes a clause that assigns representatives to "the whole number of persons in each State, excluding Indians not taxed." People were confused. Were Indigenous people U.S. citizens or not? They asked the Senate to explain the amendment. The Senate committee said the 14th Amendment did not apply to Indigenous peoples at all.

CHAPTER 4

Changing the Legal Status of Indigenous Peoples

There were some ways Indigenous people could become citizens. Under the General Allotment Act, Indigenous people could become a U.S. citizen if they accepted an allotment, or plot of land. People under a specific blood quantum, who were mostly European in ancestry, qualified for U.S. citizenship.

Indigenous women could become citizens if they married a non-Indigenous man. Sometimes, military service allowed people to become a citizen. Indigenous veterans, however, were not granted this same allowance.

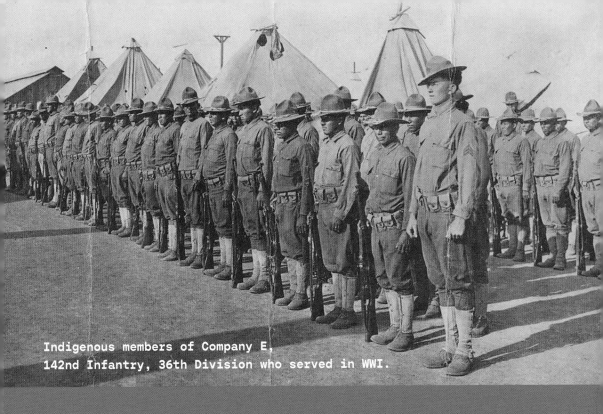

Indigenous members of Company E,
142nd Infantry, 36th Division who served in WWI.

Many Indigenous people volunteered to fight for the
U.S. in World War I. Some Indigenous groups began to
push to be granted U.S. citizenship. Other Indigenous
community members were not sure that U.S. citizenship
was a good idea. They already belonged to their
Indigenous nation and did not want to lose sight
of who they were or ownership of their traditional
Indigenous land. Still, the U.S. government began
to recognize how important Indigenous people were
to American military strength.

President Calvin Coolidge officially signed the Indian Citizenship Act on June 2, 1924. The Act allowed Indigenous people to keep their tribal affiliations.

It also allowed them to keep their rights to Indigenous property. Indigenous people almost had the same rights and privileges as any other U.S. citizen.

President Coolidge (center) poses with Indigenous delegates in 1924.

One right they still did not have, though, was the right to vote. States were in control of who could register to vote, and Indigenous people were not allowed to register. Many states, including New Mexico and Arizona, passed laws that made it illegal for Indigenous people to vote. Even after Arizona's state Supreme Court overturned one of these laws, Indigenous people continued to be kept from voting.

State election workers used the same methods that were used to disenfranchise Black voters in southern states. The Voting Rights Act of 1965 finally guaranteed the right to vote for all U.S. citizens.

The author's grandfather with the author (second from right) and her two younger siblings.

The year 1924 may seem like a long time ago, but 100 years is a short time in terms of history. It can be a short time in family history, too. For example, this book's author's grandfather was 11 years old in 1924, when he first became a U.S. citizen. Like the author, he was Indigenous. He was born in the United States, but he did not have the rights of a U.S. citizen. Indigenous people had to fight for those rights.

Indigenous Politics Today

Today, Indigenous people enjoy all the rights and privileges of being a U.S. citizen (including the right to vote), while retaining their tribal citizenship. They vote in local, state, and federal U.S. elections, as well as in their tribal elections. Tribal governments include tribal councils and tribal courts, as well as tribal presidents or other executive positions.

Indigenous voices have grown stronger in federal government in recent years. Indigenous voters turned out in large numbers to vote in the 2018 federal election. **Grassroots organizations** helped to elect the first two Indigenous women to the U.S. House of Representatives. In 2021, one of those two women, Deb Haaland, became the first Indigenous cabinet secretary. She was appointed Secretary of the Interior by President Joe Biden.

Charles Curtis was the first Indigenous congressman and senator.
He served as the 31st vice president of the United States under
Herbert Hoover until 1933.

Cabinet secretaries oversee large federal departments and serve as advisers to the president. The Bureau of Indian Affairs, along with the National Park Services, are all part of the Department of the Interior. For the first time since the U.S. was founded, an Indigenous leader oversees the protection of federal lands, resources, and cultural sites.

Deb Haaland was sworn in as Secretary of the Interior in 2021 by Vice President Kamala Harris.

Meet Deb Haaland

Debra Anne Haaland is a citizen of the Pueblo of Laguna in what is now New Mexico. Her family has lived on the land for 35 generations. Haaland's father was a U.S. Marine who served for 30 years. He earned a Silver Star Medal and saved six lives in Vietnam. Haaland's mother first served in the U.S. Navy before working in the Bureau of Indian Affairs for 25 years.

Haaland's family moved around a lot throughout her childhood. This is true of many military families. Haaland went to 13 different schools before graduating high school.

Eventually, Haaland went to law school. She served as a tribal administrator and was elected to a Board of Directors. She became the first Indigenous woman to lead a state party. Haaland is also one of the first Indigenous American women to serve in U.S. Congress. She has one child and focuses her government advocacy on matters such as environmental justice.

In 2022, for the first time in U.S. history, an Indigenous American, a Native Alaskan, and a Native Hawaiian are all serving in the U.S. House of Representatives. Due to this representation, Indigenous issues finally have a real chance of acquiring federal help. Major issues such as returning land to Indigenous nations, the crisis of missing and murdered Indigenous women, and providing clean water to Indigenous communities may at last receive the attention they deserve.

The fight to protect Indigenous water supplies and land rights continues.

Activists work to bring attention to missing and murdered Indigenous women, refusing to let them be forgotten.

In 1924, Indigenous people became United States citizens, but that did not mean that life became easy for them. Indigenous people continued to fight to be heard and recognized as sovereign nations. Their fight for respect is one they will not give up on and which continues today. The rest of the U.S. needs to realize that Indigenous people are here to stay.

EXTEND YOUR LEARNING

BOOKS

Friedman, Mark. *The Democratic Process: Cornerstones of Freedom*. Children's Press, Danbury, CT, 2011.

Loh-Hagan, Virgina. *Stand Up, Speak Out: Indigenous Rights*. 45th Parallel Press, Ann Arbor, MI, 2022.

Mendoza, Brenda Perez. *What Is a Dreamer? / ¿Qué es un Soñador?* Cherry Lake Press, Ann Arbor, MI, 2023.

Winn, Kevin. *What Is Democracy?* Cherry Lake Press, Ann Arbor, MI, 2023.

WEBSITES

With an adult, learn more online with these suggested searches.

"Indigenous People of the Americans (original inhabitants of the Americans)," Britannica Kids.

"National Museum of the American Indian," Smithsonian.

"Tribal Nations & the United States: An Introduction," National Congress of American Indians.

"Voting Rights for Native Americans," Library of Congress.

GLOSSARY

blood quantum (BLUHD KWAHN-tuhm) the amount of tribal affiliation in a person's ancestry

charters (CHAR-tuhrz) documents that give rights to a group

citizenship (SI-tuh-zuhn-ship) legally belonging to a certain community

colonizing (KAH-luh-nie-zing) the taking over of another nation's land and resources, usually through use of force

deported (di-PORT-uhd) officially removed from a country

disenfranchise (dis-in-FRAN-chiez) withhold the right to vote

General Allotment Act (JEN-ruhl uh-LAHT-muhnt AKT) an act of Congress that divided reservations into sections and assigned pieces of the land to individual registered tribal members

generations (jen-uh-RAY-shuhns) populations living during the same time period

grassroots organizations (GRAS-roots or-guh-nuh-ZAY-shuhns) local collective groups with a shared purpose

Indian Removal Act (IN-dee-uhn ri-MOO-vuhl AKT) a congressional act from 1830 that gave the president power to set aside land west of the Mississippi River for eastern tribal nations; began the reservation system and was the basis for forceful removal

kinship (KIN-ship) relationship

sovereignty (SAH-vruhn-tee) independence to self-govern

treaty (TREE-tee) an official agreement between two nations

visa (VEE-zuh) a formal document granting permission to enter or remain in a country

INDEX

American Revolution (1775-1783), 12

citizenship
Indigenous/tribal, 8, 10, 21–23, 26
U.S., defining, 4, 6, 19, 20
U.S., denied to Indigenous, 6, 15, 17, 18, 19, 25
U.S., for Indigenous, 5, 20–24, 25, 26
U.S., rights and privileges, 4–6, 17, 18, 24, 25, 26

civil rights
for all, 4, 6
for citizens, 4–5, 17, 18, 24
colonization, 10–11, 16–17

Congress
Indigenous representatives, 26, 30
laws and policy history, 14–18, 19, 20, 22–24

Constitution of the United States, 4, 18, 19
Coolidge, Calvin, 22–23
court cases, 17–18, 24
Curtis, Charles, 27

democracies, 7, 19
Department of the Interior, 26, 28, 29
deportation, 5

enslaved people, 6
environmental justice, 29, 30
European settlers, 9, 10–11, 20

federal benefits, 5
federal jobs, 5, 26–30
14th Amendment, 19

General Allotment Act (1887), 16–18, 20
government structures, 7, 8, 13

Haaland, Deb, 26, 28–29
Harris, Kamala, 28
Haudenosaunee peoples, 13

Indian Citizenship Act (1924), 22–23, 31
Indian Removal Act (1830), 14–15

Indigenous people
culture and modern life, 13, 15, 25, 31
history, 8–13, 14–18, 25
in modern politics, 26–30, 31
tribal citizenship, 8, 10, 21–23
U.S. citizenship, 5, 20–24, 25, 26
U.S. citizenship denied, 6, 15, 17, 18, 19, 25

juries, 6

land policies, 10–12, 14–18, 20, 28, 30
Lenape people, 14, 15

Massasoit, 9
matrilineal organization, 8, 13
military service, 20–21, 29
missing and murdered Indigenous women, 30, 31

Oklahoma Land Rush (1889), 16–17
Onondaga Nation, 13

passports, 5
politicians, modern Indigenous, 26–30
powwows, 15
religious freedom, 18
representative democracy, 7, 19
reservation lands, 14–18

Shenandoah, Audrey, 13
sovereignty, 14, 18, 31
state laws, 24

trade, 10, 11
treaties, 13, 14–15

voting rights
Indigenous, 13, 17, 24, 26
United States, 4–5, 7, 17, 24, 26
Voting Rights Act (1965), 24

Wampanoag Nation, 9
women, 8, 13, 20, 30, 31
World War I, 21